# EXPLORERS!

# Marco Polo
## Explorer of China

*Kathy Feeney*

**Enslow Publishers, Inc.**

40 Industrial Road      PO Box 38
Box 398      Aldershot
Berkeley Heights, NJ 07922    Hants GU12 6BP
USA      UK

http://www.enslow.com

**Library of Congress Cataloging-in-Publication Data**

Feeney, Kathy, 1954-
    Marco Polo : explorer of China / Kathy Feeney.
        p. cm. — (Explorers!)
    Summary: Introduces the life and accomplishments of Italian explorer
Marco Polo, who journeyed to Asia in the 1200s, became friends with
Kublai Khan, ruler of the Mongolian Empire, and served him as an
official messenger to other nations.
    Includes bibliographical references and index.
    ISBN 0-7660-2145-9
    1. Polo, Marco, 1254-1323?—Travel—Juvenile literature. 2. Explorers—
Italy—Biography—Juvenile literature. 3. Travel, Medieval—Juvenile literature.
4. Asia—Description and travel—Juvenile literature. [1. Polo, Marco, 1254-1323?
2. Explorers. 3. Voyages and travels. 4. Asia—Description and travel.] I. Title.
II. Explorers! (Enslow Publishers)
G370.P9F44 2004
910.4—dc21

                        2003014780

Printed in the United States of America

10 9 8 7 6 5 4 3 2 1

**To Our Readers:** We have done our best to make sure all Internet Addresses in this book were active and appropriate when we went to press. However, the author and the publisher have no control over and assume no liability for the material available on those Internet sites or on other Web sites they may link to. Any comments or suggestions can be sent by e-mail to comments@enslow.com or to the address on the back cover.

# Contents

List of Maps

| Map | Page |
| --- | --- |
| China | 4 |
| Marco Polo's Route | 19 |
| Asia | 29 |

Marco Polo told amazing stories of his journey through China. This map shows what China looks like today.

N
W        E
S

Beijing

Shanghai

Xi'an

CHINA

Guangzhou

TAIWAN

Hong Kong

# The Travels of Marco Polo

Marco Polo lived what some people thought was an unbelievable life. In 1271, Marco left his hometown of Venice, Italy, for the first time. He went with his father and uncle to a land called China. The Polos had to travel across snowy mountains, deserts, and rivers. They traveled nearly 12,000 miles. It took them three years just to reach China.

Marco Polo lived during a time when some people thought the world was flat. They thought that if they traveled too far, they could fall right off the earth.

Airplanes, trains, and cars had not been invented. People traveled by foot, boat, on horseback, and camel.

People believed the world was flat and
if you sailed too far you would fall off
the edge. Some people thought the
world was on columns.

Trips were difficult and dangerous. But that did not scare
Marco Polo. He went where few Europeans had ever
been. Marco Polo knew there were wonderful new lands
waiting to be explored.

Marco Polo wrote about his first time seeing a giraffe

when he visited the island of Zanzibar: "In this country is found also the giraffe or cameleopard, which is a handsome beast. The body is well-proportioned, the fore-legs long and high, the hind-legs short, the neck very long, the head small, and in its manners it is gentle."

In Marco Polo's time, no one believed such creatures as a giraffe existed.

When Marco Polo was dying, some people still did not believe he had seen the wonders he told about. They thought he had made up the people and places in his book. And they told him to admit that he had lied.

But, Marco Polo said, "I have not told half of what I saw."

Marco Polo spent much of his time at the port in Venice. There he learned how to be a merchant.

# Growing Up in Venice

Marco Polo was born in Venice, Italy, in 1254. His father was a merchant. There is not much known about his mother.

When Marco was six, his father, Nicolo, and his uncle, Maffeo, left Venice. Venice was an important port city. Ships from Asia, Europe, North Africa, and India docked there. The Polos traveled to another country known as Cathay. This country is now the northern part of China.

China was as different to Europeans as Mars is today to people on Earth. The Polo brothers traded jewels for treasures from China to sell in Europe. Gold and jewels

Jade was traded between Venice and China. Jade is a hard, green stone that is made into jewelry and carved ornaments.

were traded for pearls, silk, jade, and tea.

Marco's mother died while his father was in China. Marco lived with an aunt and uncle in Venice. In school, Marco learned to read and how to add and subtract. He also learned Italian and French. He learned about religion and about being a Roman Catholic.

Marco liked to find out about things, and he liked to watch people and animals. He enjoyed hearing about new places. When he was not in school, Marco learned about the world at the city's port. He watched ships sail into the busy port. They were loaded with riches from around the world. Marco met merchants who had returned to Venice with items such as silk and spices.

Spices are made from the bark, buds, flowers, seeds, and other parts of certain plants and trees. Spices can make some foods look and smell more interesting. Many people use spices to make food taste better. Pepper, nutmeg, and cinnamon are some popular spices. European merchants also traded with the Chinese for salt.

**Spices hid the taste of spoiling food.**

Marco Polo heard about people who made silk from the cocoons of special worms.

There were no refrigerators back then and food spoiled easily. Salt helped keep food from getting rotten.

The men told tales of bad storms and battles with pirates. They told stories about seeing mermaids in the sea. The merchants told about people who made silk from the cocoon of a worm and divers who harvested pearls from shellfish called oysters.

The merchants told Marco about a whole new world outside of Venice. He wanted to go and see everything himself.

Then, in 1269, his father and uncle returned home to Venice. Marco was fifteen. His life was about to change.

Marco Polo was always interested in the stories merchants told him. He heard stories of people diving for pearls.

Marco Polo's father and uncle meet the emperor Kublai Khan.

# A Teenage Traveler

Two years after his father and uncle returned to Venice, Marco packed his clothes. He was going with them to Asia. Marco was seventeen when he began what is now a very famous trip.

During their first trip to China, Nicolo and Maffeo Polo had met with Kublai Khan. The emperor wanted to learn more about Europe and the people who lived there. The Polos told the Khan about the pope. He was the head of the Roman Catholic Church. The Khan asked the Polos to return to Italy to invite a hundred men of the Christian faith to China. The emperor told them

## Kublai Khan

Kublai Khan was born in 1215 and died in 1294. He was the founder of the Mongol Empire in China. The Khan was the emperor of China from 1259 to 1294.

Kublai Khan's grandfather, Genghis Khan, was a famous warrior. His father, Ogodie, was a famous conqueror. Kublai Khan was a brave warrior as well as a smart ruler.

Kublai Khan was a great military leader. And he was also known for being smart. The Mongols called him Setsen Khan, which means "The Wise Khan." When Kublai Khan became the ruler of China, he made many changes. He organized farmers into groups of fifty families. These groups worked together to plant trees, water crops, and control floods. Storage bins for grain were filled so everyone would have enough to eat. Kublai Khan liked to learn, and he was interested in other countries. He liked to meet people from different places. Marco Polo was one of many merchants who was welcomed by the Khan and was asked to work for him.

**Kublai Khan was a good leader who was respected by the people he ruled.**

he and his people wanted to learn about Christianity.

When they returned to Italy, the Polos could not find a hundred Christian men to go with them to China. The pope told two monks to make the trip with the Polos.

The men packed food, clothing, and medicine. They brought jewels to trade. They also carried letters and gifts from the pope.

The three Polos and two monks sailed from Venice in the summer of

Kublai Khan was eager to learn about Roman Catholics and the pope. This is St. Peter's Basilica in Rome.

1271. The travelers started their trip by ship and continued by land. The trip was not easy. They were

Marco Polo began his voyage to the distant land of China from the port of Venice.

often hungry. Sometimes they came across dangerous animals and people who were at war.

Partway through the trip, the monks got scared. They turned around and went home. Three years after they had sailed from Venice, the Polos finally reached China in 1274.

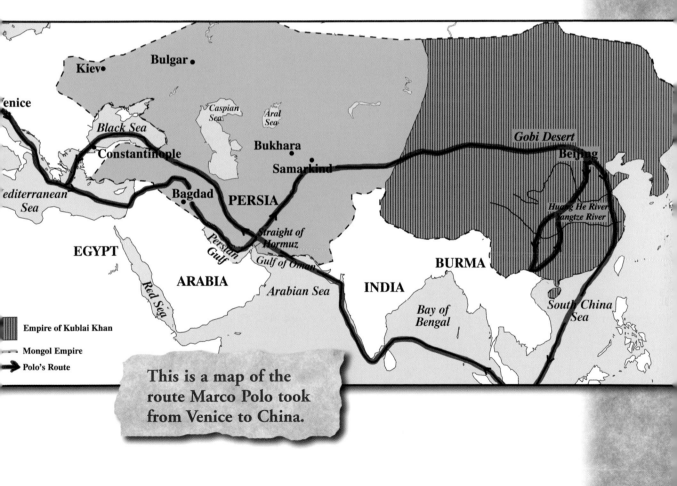

**Empire of Kublai Khan**

**Mongol Empire**

**Polo's Route**

This is a map of the route Marco Polo took from Venice to China.

The Polos followed trails, roads, and went through mountain passes. They even had to cross rivers.

# The Journey to China

Once the Polos landed on the continent of Asia, they followed ancient roads, trails, and mountain passes. These roads connected the Far East with the West. Today that route is called the Silk Road. It is named for the treasure and silk the early merchants risked their lives to get. At that time, China was the only place where the cocoons of the silkworm were woven into silk. Traders returning to Europe with silk could become rich. They traveled together to stay safe. The Polos went by foot, horse, camel, and yak. They crossed rivers in big boats powered by men rowing oars.

The Polos used many different animals to travel, such as yaks.

The travelers passed through Armenia to Persia. From Persia they went to Badakhahan. Persia is now known as Iran. Marco became ill in the cold mountains. The Polos waited for a year until Marco was feeling better.

Once Marco was well enough to travel, the Polos continued through the Pamir Mountains in central Asia. Marco kept notes during the trip. He said the mountains were where no birds would fly. The mountains were very high, and the air very cold.

After nearly two months, the Polos had crossed the Pamir Mountains. They were now on a big plain in western China. The Polos stopped in the cities Kashgar and Yarkand.

They climbed steep mountains and walked through deep snow. Heavy rains turned some of the roads they traveled into mud. Next, they had to cross the southern section of the Gobi desert. The desert was very hot.

**The Polos had to cross the Pamir Mountains.**

The Gobi was a difficult part of the journey because of the hot temperatures and strong winds.

Sometimes the Polos battled sandstorms. They traveled through the dry, sandy land until they reached a place where the men could stop to rest. They found an oasis, which is a green area in the middle of the desert with plants and water. At night, the desert was as cold as it was hot during the day.

The Chinese called the Gobi "The Flowing Sands." The nickname came from the fact that strong winds blew all the time, changing the shape of the sand. Travelers were warned not to listen to the whispering sound the sands made. Many of them thought the noise sounded like voices that came from ghosts.

Marco wrote that the "voices" sometimes made travelers go off their path. "And in this way many travelers have been lost and have perished," he wrote. Once they were safely across the Gobi, the Polos wanted to meet with Kublai Khan.

## From Marco Polo's *Il milione*

"It is asserted as a well-known fact that this desert is the abode [home] of many evil spirits, which amuse travellers . . . If, during the daytime, any persons remain behind on the road, either when overtaken by sleep . . . until the caravan has passed a hill and is no longer in sight, they unexpectedly hear themselves called to by their names, and in tone of voice to which they are accustomed."

Marco Polo met emperor Kublai
Khan in China. The two men
became good friends.

# Exploring the East

In 1275, Marco Polo met Kublai Khan, the ruler of the Mongol Empire. He was probably the most important person Marco would ever know. The Khan ruled over lands that are now Mongolia, China, Russia, and Iran.

The Polos went to the Khan's summer palace in Shangdu, near what is today Kalgan. Kublai Khan had riches few Europeans had ever seen. Thousands of guards watched over him. His palace had walls covered with gold and silver. It was decorated with carved dragons and paintings of animals and battles. His stables

### From Marco Polo's *Il milione*

Marco Polo wrote about some of the things Kublai Khan did while the Polos were visiting.

"Frequently, when he [Kublai Khan] rides about this enclosed forest, he has one or more small leopards carried on horseback, behind their keepers; and when he pleases to give direction for their being slipped, they instantly seize a stag, or goat, or fallow deer, which he gives to his hawks, and in this manner he amuses himself."

housed a thousand white horses. The Khan had four wives and twenty-two sons.

The powerful Chinese emperor and Marco Polo became good friends. Kublai Khan liked Marco because he was smart and wanted to find out everything. Marco was good at telling what he saw by writing about it.

He liked the emperor's interest in learning. When Marco wrote about the Khan he said: "His complexion [skin] is fair and ruddy like a rose, the eyes black and handsome, the nose shapely and set squarely in place."

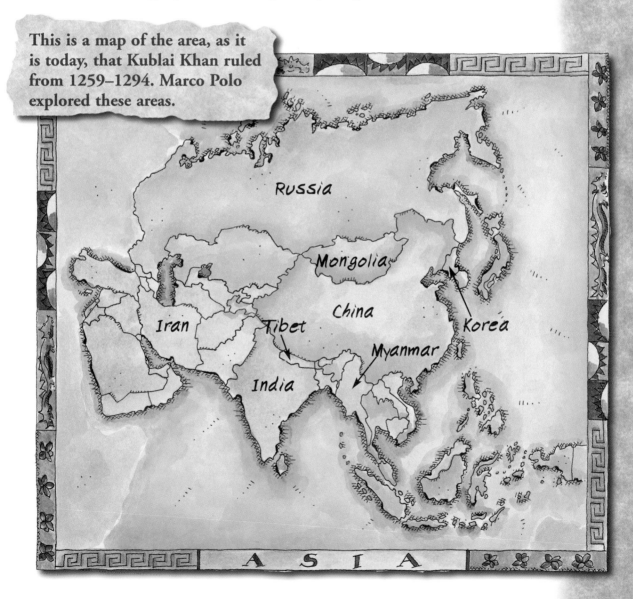

This is a map of the area, as it is today, that Kublai Khan ruled from 1259–1294. Marco Polo explored these areas.

Russia

Mongolia

China

Iran

Tibet

Korea

Myanmar

India

A S I A

Marco Polo saw a crocodile for the first time during his travels.

Kublai Khan made Marco a messenger in his court. The people of China were told to call him Master Marco Polo. He was sent on official trips to Burma (now Myanmar), Korea, Tibet, and India.

Marco saw many wonders in the East. Everywhere he traveled, he took notes to share with Kublai Khan. In India, Marco watched divers hold their breaths for a very long time. When they came up from the bottom of the sea, the men had harvested oysters. Sometimes the oysters would have precious pearls in them.

He learned languages such as Persian, Turkish, and Mongolian. He tasted a nut "the size of a man's head and as white as milk." It was called a coconut. Marco ate a fruit called a date that grew on a palm tree. He tasted spices like nutmeg and ginger that were used to flavor food.

Marco saw a crocodile for the first time. He noted that it had jaws wide enough to eat and swallow a man.

He saw silver and gold palaces. He saw soldiers ride elephants into battle.

Many men would dive for oysters in hopes of finding a pearl inside.

The people in Asia rode into battle on elephants rather than horses.

Marco saw people use paper money instead of coins. "With these pieces of paper they can buy anything and pay for anything," he wrote.

Marco saw grass called bamboo that grew as tall as

trees. He saw bamboo spears used to scare away tigers, money made from cakes of salt, and gold pagodas. A pagoda has several levels and looks like a tower. It is made of stone, brick, or wood. The pagodas Marco Polo saw were built to honor the Buddhist religion. Today, people sometimes use pagodas to decorate a garden.

After spending many years in China, the Polos decided to go back to Venice.

**This is what a town in China might have looked like. The tall towers are called pagodas.**

Venice had grown in the time Marco Polo was away.

This is the warship that Marco Polo used while fighting for control over the Mediterranean Sea.

# Il milione

The Polos returned to Venice in 1295. Marco Polo was forty-one. His trip had taken twenty-four years. He had left Venice as a teen and was now a man.

Venice had also grown. There were buildings Polo had never seen and streets he did not know. Venice and Genoa had become enemies. The cities were fighting over who would control the Mediterranean Sea.

Polo became a commander in the Venetian navy. He was captured by the enemies and sent to prison in Genoa. There, Polo met another prisoner named Rustichello. He was a writer from Pisa, Italy. Polo and

Marco Polo used his time in prison to tell the stories of his travels, while his friend, Rustichello, wrote them down.

Rustichello shared a prison cell. During their time together, Polo told Rustichello stories of his adventures in China.

Rustichello had an idea. Polo could make his memories into a book. The two friends worked together.

During their year together, Polo told his story while Rustichello wrote it down on paper. With the help of his writer friend, Polo's book was called *Description of the World*. It was commonly called *Il milione*.

His book told Europeans about things they had never seen. Polo told how Kublai Khan lived in palaces with beds covered by silk sheets. He told about oil as

From Marco Polo's *Il milione*

Marco Polo told how Kublai Khan and his subjects used coal to heat water for bathing.

"It is true that they have plenty of firewood, too. But the population is so enormous and there are so many bath-houses and baths constantly being heated, that it would be impossible to supply enough firewood . . . so these stones [coal], being very plentiful and very cheap, effect a great saving of wood."

"a substance spurting from the ground and used for burning in lamps."

Marco Polo told about the mail system in China. Kublai Khan had come up with a way for people to communicate quickly. Messages were carried across his empire and delivered by horseback riders. Each messenger would ride about twenty-five miles to a relay station. There he would pass the message on to a new

Marco Polo returned to the port in Venice and became a merchant.

Christopher Columbus was an explorer who believed Marco Polo's stories. He went on a voyage of his own to discover new lands.

rider on a fresh horse. These riders could cover about 250 miles a day.

Polo was set free from prison around 1299. He worked as a merchant and became rich. He married and had three daughters.

Most people read Polo's story. They thought he was the first European to travel across Asia and write about

This is Venice today. Marco Polo is buried at the Church of San Lorenzo.

## The Age of Exploration

Many people read Marco Polo's book and wanted to explore. The 1400s to the 1800s were considered the Age of Exploration. Many great discoveries were being made at this time. Explorers like Christopher Columbus and Ferdinand Magellan had sailed the seas. In 1492, Columbus made his first voyage and found lands in the Caribbean Sea. In 1519, Magellan started his voyage. He was the first to lead a voyage around the world.

In Europe during this time, many men were searching for a way to get to the Indies by crossing the oceans. The countries of India, China, Japan, and the East Indies were know as the Indies. Spices and silk goods were brought to Europe from the Indies over dangerous land routes. Reaching the Indies by water would mean the men and their country would become very rich.

**Marco Polo wrote about the silk he saw in China. In the sixteenth century, silk goods were brought to tailor shops. There the silk was made into clothing or other items.**

what he saw. Christopher Columbus believed Marco Polo. Columbus and other explorers started their own trips to find new lands and riches.

Others did not believe Marco Polo had seen the things he talked about. He was called "Il Milione," meaning Marco Millions. Marco Polo might have been given that name because he was a millionaire. It could also be because people thought his millions of stories were made up. Some thought that the pictures in the book were not real. Some of the artists who drew the pictures made up things that Polo did not talk about. One picture showed a man with one leg and a big foot. He was using his foot like a beach umbrella to shade himself from the sun.

Marco Polo died on January 9, 1324, at seventy years of age. Polo was buried in the Church of San Lorenzo in Venice. He left a large sum of money for his family. And he left stories of a land few Europeans had ever seen. Marco Polo has left many people wondering what else he could have seen and written about.

# Timeline

**1254**—Marco Polo is born in Venice, Italy.

**1259**—Kublai Khan becomes the ruler of the Mongol Empire.

**1269**—Marco's father and uncle return from China.

**1271**—Marco begins the journey to China with his father and uncle.

**1275**—Marco meets Kublai Khan.

**1292**—The Polos leave China to return home to Venice.

**1294**—Kublai Khan dies.

**1295**—The Polos arrive in Venice.

**1298**—Marco Polo is sent to prison during the war between Venice and Genoa; tells his story to a writer while in prison; publishes *Il milione*.

**January 9, 1324**—Marco Polo dies.

# Words to Know

**ancient**—Very old.

**Asia**—The largest continent in the world.

**Cathay**—The name for northern China during Marco Polo's time.

**cocoon**—A silky covering that caterpillars make around them. This protects them as they change into butterflies or moths.

**commander**—The officer in charge.

**continent**—A very large body of land. The continents of the world are Asia, Africa, Europe, North America, South America, Antarctica, and Australia.

**emperor**—The ruler of a country.

**merchant**—A person who buys and sells things.

**palace**—The home of a ruler, usually a large house.

**pirate**—A robber who travels by ship.

**village**—A small area of land where people settle. Villages are smaller than towns.

# Learn More About
# Marco Polo

## Books

Brandon, Alex. *The Travels of Marco Polo*. New York: Raintree Steck-Vaughn Publishers, 2000.

Burgan, Michael. *Marco Polo and the Silk Road to China*. Mankato, Minn.: Compass Point Books, 2002.

Herbert, Janis. *Marco Polo for Kids: His Marvelous Journey to China*. Chicago, Ill.: Chicago Review Press, 2001.

MacDonald, Fiona. *The World in the Time of Marco Polo*. Broomall, Penn.: Chelsea House Publishers, 2000.

Major, John S. *The Silk Route*. New York: HarperTrophy, 1996.

# Internet Addresses

**Marco Polo: Explorer**

<http://www.enchantedlearning.com/explorers/page/
p/polo.shtml>

*Learn more about Marco Polo from this Enchanted Learning site.*

**In the Footsteps of Marco Polo**

<http://www.metmuseum.org/explore/Marco/index.html>

*Follow Marco Polo's journey to China with this site from the Metropolitan Museum of Art.*

# Index